The Devil's Bagpipe:
The True Life of Martin Luther
(1581)

by
JAMES LAING
Translated by Fr. Robert Nixon, OSB

SENSUS FIDELIUM
PRESS

Translated by Fr. Robert Nixon, OSB

ISBN: 978-1-962639-42-2

Book Cover, Interior, and E-book Design by
Amit Dey | amitdey2528@gmail.com
For more information, please visit sensusfideliumpress.com

Protestantism, or 'the reformed religion,' as its founders haughtily call it, is the sum of all heresies that ever existed before it, that have arisen since, or that may arise hereafter for the ruin of souls.

Pope Pius X

Table of Contents

Translator's Note

It is fair to say that most Catholics have only a somewhat vague idea of the life and career of Martin Luther. We are perhaps familiar with the image of a sincere and zealous but unfortunately misguided member of the Order of St. Augustine, whose conscience was troubled with issues of sin, salvation, and faith. Following the popular version of this narrative, these theological concerns led Luther to nail his ninety-five theses on the door of a church at Wittenberg—an incident which most scholars now agree is an entirely apocryphal event, invented by Protestant imaginations in later centuries. The concerns raised by Luther (so the story goes) caused widespread and profound issues relating to theology and ecclesiology to come to a decisive head, leading to unfortunate and long-lasting divisions within the Western Church.

However, an examination of the early sources reveals the truth of the situation to be very different. One such early source of particular value and importance is *De vita et moribus atque rebus gestis haereticorum nostri temporis* ("The Life, Conduct, and Deeds of the Heretics of our

Times"), written by a learned and devout Scotsman, James Laing. This work was published in Latin in 1581, but penned some years before, originally in the French language. Laing is described, even in Protestant sources, as a reputable and diligent historian and "possessing a most excellent genius in Letters." Having moved to France as a young student, he went on to serve as a Professor of Theology at both the Universities of Sorbonne and of Paris.

There are several compelling reasons to give the firmest credence to Laing's work on the life of Luther. Firstly, it is one of the earliest extant biographies of Luther, being written only about three decades after his death, when the real facts and series of events were still widely known to the public and readily verifiable by anyone who was interested. Laing, born in 1499, had actually lived through the events in question, and would hardly have falsified his account of Luther's actions, many of which took place in a very public arena and were still matters of official record and general public knowledge.

Secondly, the 1581 Latin version was published with the full approval and authorization of the Faculty of the University of Paris. This venerable body, staffed by the very best scholars from all of Western Europe, would certainly not endorse any work of dubious veracity, even if it was overtly pro-Catholic. While the University of Paris was itself a Catholic institution, the standing of its scholarship was such that it was firmly committed to objective truth in matters of historical research.

Thirdly, the author himself is clearly trying to be as balanced and fair as possible, and openly acknowledges in some instances talents on the part of Luther, and also failings (and sometimes very embarrassing failings) on the part of orthodox Catholics.[1] In the very few instances where he introduces legends or unverified rumors which were in circulation at the time, he openly acknowledges them to be such. Moreover, whenever Laing is uncertain of a fact (such as the precise details of Luther's death) he openly confesses his uncertainty—something which a partisan historian would hardly be inclined to do, unless he had genuine regard for veracity.

Laing's work presents several challenges to the translator. Firstly, proper names are given in Latinized versions, and the formation of these Latin names is very far from consistent. In the present translation, names are given in the most commonly used vernacular forms (although the German spellings also often exhibit a bewildering variability). Where the original text includes only the surname, or (in a few cases) only the Christian name, of an individual, the full version of the name has been inserted, at least in the initial instance.

---

[1] An example of this is the encouragement of Luther in his objections to indulgences misguidedly given to him by his religious superior at the time, Fr. Johann von Staupitz, OSA.

Footnotes providing brief biographical information on the characters named in the text has been provided throughout. The exception to this is for popes, emperors and dukes, since the details of their lives are very readily available in other sources.

No chapter divisions, or even paragraph spacings, are given in the original edition. The present chapter titles, together with the paragraph divisions, are thus all the work of the translator. Hopefully, they will serve to make the work easier to follow and more accessible for the contemporary reader.

Finally, Laing frequently uses irony, hyperbole and other rhetorical devices of expression. In most cases, an effort has been made to retain these in the translation. In the few cases where it has not been possible to convey the intended meaning in idiomatic English, this has been noted in footnotes. Texts which are editorial insertion are indicated throughout by means of square brackets, thus: [....].

In the following pages, we read about an ambitious Luther trying to obtain for himself the dignity of the cardinalate at a young age. We learn about the true motives for his objections to indulgences, which sprang principally from resentment at the loss of income for his own Augustinian Order. We witness also his bad temper and vitriolic tongue, his nocturnal conversations with demons (whether they were real or imagined), and his scandalous and degrading bouts of drunkenness and debauchery. The title given here for this biography, *The Devil's Bagpipe*, was suggested by a striking woodcut image produced in 1535 by Erhard Schoen, and reproduced on the cover of this volume.

This is a work which all Catholics (and indeed, all people interested in history) should read, for it substantially modifies and corrects the popular but inaccurate "myth" of Luther, replacing it with a more balanced, credible and truthful account of the life, character and motives of a man who gravely distorted the Gospel of Christ and did untold damage to His one true Catholic Church.

Fr. Robert Nixon, OSB
Abbey of the Most Holy Trinity,
New Norcia, Western Australia

I.
Luther's Early Life, Education and Entrance into the Augustinian Order

Martin Luther, as he himself attests in one of his sermons on the Eucharist, was born in a certain town called Eisleben, in the county of Mansfeld, in the diocese of Albastat in Saxony. He was born into this world on the night before the feast day of St. Martin, and it was this fact which prompted his parents to assign to him this name (which was then highly celebrated and esteemed in the Catholic, apostolic and Roman Church) when he was baptized, in the Year of Our Lord 1483.

The name of his father was Hans Luder. Now, "Luder" was a surname held in the greatest possible disdain and contempt by the Germans, for in that language it means "whore." In order that his son might avoid the shame of bearing this unfortunate surname, Hans determined that the infant should be known, not as "Martin Luder," but rather as "Martin Luther." And the name of his mother was Margarita.

A story circulated by many reputable and respectable persons is that before Margarita and Hans were united in marriage, a certain evil spirit would often appear to the unmarried maiden in the guise of a remarkably handsome youth. This evil spirit, disguised in this manner, successfully seduced her and, having gained her affections, and would secretly lie with her—and thus Martin Luther, the future schismatic and mortal foe of the Faith, came to be conceived. Thus, according to this story, he was not only fathered out of wedlock, but spawned by the embraces of an infernal demon!

Regardless of the veracity or otherwise of this legend, it is clear that his parents were utterly undistinguished individuals with respect to personal merit and reputation, being wholly devoid of any splendor or credit of life or virtue. Moreover, it is clear that their son was conceived out of wedlock.

Nevertheless, being driven by ambition, they had Martin, who was their only child, study diligently the first elements of grammar at Eisleben. Very soon afterwards, they sent him to Magdeburg for the purpose of continuing his schooling. There, he completed a full year of foundational education.

Following this, Martin proceeded to Eisenach, where a teacher was engaged for him who instructed him for some four years. During this time, he was immersed primarily in the study of the humanities. Yet he applied himself also to the study of philosophy, through his own initiative.

Martin became convinced that he could advance more readily and easily in these philosophical studies if he moved to Erfurt. For that town, with its prestigious university, enjoyed a very great reputation, and was the most celebrated center of learning in all of the German province of Thuringia. There (at least in his own estimation) Martin very quickly became the expert in all the literary arts and progressed with equal rapidity in his philosophical studies. And so, at the age of about twenty, he obtained his Master of Arts degree.

Thus, at this early point in his life, Martin had already experienced a considerable amount of praise and adulation on account of his success as a scholar. He had acquired a taste for this recognition and praise, and felt that, in respect to cleverness and intelligence, he easily excelled all of his peers. And so, driven on by a thirst for personal advancement and fame, and placing faith in his own abilities and ingenuity, he next began to study law.

In this new field of study, and whatever else pertained to erudition, he took the greatest efforts to display to others his talents, both in speech-making and disputation. It must be acknowledged that, at first, the life he led was not altogether dissipated and given over to vices, for he was at that time undeniably diligent and industrious.

It is a part of human nature that, when afflicted by the fatigue resulting from toil and concentrated labor, a person typically seeks refuge and recreation through activities of quiet leisure. It was likewise with the young Martin Luther. After long hours of study, he would sometimes give himself over to bouts of relaxation to restore his energies. And so, one day he went for a long walk through the peaceful meadows of the countryside, accompanied by one of his friends.

Now, although the weather had been perfectly clement and serene until that moment, all of a sudden, a blazing lightning bolt descended from the sky! It struck Martin's companion directly, and that hapless young man met his death instantaneously. Martin himself, however, though utterly shocked and shaken, was entirely unharmed.

His reaction to this untoward and calamitous event was one of morbid terror. In the days and nights that followed he would often be seized with fits of shivering and chills generated by the mortal horror which had seized upon his heart. As with many people who are made acutely aware of their own mortality and the fragility and ephemerality of this earthly existence, Luther's mind turned to thoughts of religion and eternity. Thus, he resolved to abandon all pleasures and amusements of the flesh and the world, and to join a religious order and consecrate himself completely to God.

Those who had known Martin for any length of time, however, were completely surprised by this resolution—or rather, impulse. For they had hitherto witnessed nothing whatsoever of piety or devotion in his life or conduct and could hardly believe that he could successfully put into practice this decision to live in a monastic cloister.

Notwithstanding this, he chose to enter the venerable Order of St. Augustine. That great order is celebrated throughout the world for the austerity of life of its members, and their strict cultivation of solitude and silence. Indeed, at the beginning of his religious life, Martin behaved with almost exemplary dedication and discipline, and completed his first year without reproach in the monastery of the Augustinians in Erfurt. For the next four years of his religious life, he continued to conduct himself in a diligent and studious manner, without giving rise to any serious scandal.

But around that time, and little by little, his monastic confreres began to observe (I cannot say by what particular sign or specific indication in his behavior or appearance) that something was seriously amiss with Martin. They were led to conclude that either he was afflicted by some underlying and unsettling illness of mind or body, or that he had fallen prey to some secret and insidious vice of the soul, or that he was under the influence of some malign demon or evil spirit with which he was holding occult and clandestine communications.

The matter brought itself to a head one day, in a very striking fashion. For once when the divine liturgy of the Mass was being celebrated, the Gospel for the day was read, which happened to be the passage from the seventh chapter of Mark which describes a man possessed by a certain deaf and dumb spirit.[2] At the very moment when these Gospel words were being read, Martin fell to the ground, face down. And he cried out loudly in a most horrible voice, "It is not I! It is not I!"

Whatever may be concluded from this well-attested incident, it is certain that Luther himself has declared quite publicly that he had personally been acquainted with an evil spirit, and that the same evil spirit had likewise known him. He also said, metaphorically, that he had supped with such a malign entity, and (using an old German proverb) that he and this evil spirit had eaten "more than a little salt" together.

There is also a notorious book in existence on the Mass, which Luther wrote while hidden away in one of the corners of the monastery, in the German language. This dreadful book is sufficient to persuade us conclusively of his communication with demonic entities. For he relates to the reader nocturnal conversations he held with this

---

[2] See Mark 7:31-37.

evil spirit regarding the propriety of offering of the sacrifice of the Mass with no congregation present.[3]

See now, O Reader, the foundations of this newly-invented "fifth Gospel," which this new species of heretic, who himself was taught his theology by a demon, presents to us—which, indeed, he would impose upon us and shove down our throats! Ask yourself, O good Reader, is it likely or credible that Jesus Christ would wish His holy message to be preached and proclaimed by such a wretched man as this, who was clearly (at best) a disturbed and unbalanced fanatic, or (more likely) actually possessed by an evil spirit?

This may perhaps seem to you to be but a small objection to his doctrine, but we shall proceed further, to examine more fully the nefarious effects of this "new Gospel" of Martin Luther.

---

[3] In his writings and sermons, Luther frequently declared himself to have had frequent interactions and conversations with devils, and related how, during his years in the Augustinian monastery, an evil spirit would assault him at night. This spirit, he said, attacked him physically, mentally and spiritually.

Figure 1: *Martin Luther conversing with a devil*,
Woodcut, Leipzig, 1535.

II.
Luther's Academic Career, and his Attempt to be Appointed as a Cardinal

Around those times, the University of Wittenberg was established by Frederick, the Duke of Saxony. This Duke Frederick was one of those nobles vested with power in the election of the Holy Roman Emperor.[4] The foundation of this new academic institution became the opportunity for Martin Luther to circulate more widely his recently invented heresies.

In the Year of our Lord 1508, Luther was appointed a teacher of philosophy at the University of Wittenberg. Whether it was on account of his youthfulness, or the "great authority" of this young teacher (as he would have it), or the splendor and beauty of the ancient city

---

[4] This was Frederick III, who ruled the Electorate of Saxony from 1486-1525. He was a protector and support of Martin Luther, but remained a Catholic himself.

of Wittenberg, or simply the newness of the university, a great multitude of students flocked to hear him.

Having been thus established in his academic position, this new teacher, Luther, became bolder and more arrogant than ever. He was also (at least in his own eyes!) more learned than anyone else—for such pride is indeed a trait which is typical of all heretics. Nevertheless, for the first three years he carried out his duties with sufficient diligence and propriety, and in an effective and commendable fashion.

Meanwhile, there were some seven monasteries of the Order of St. Augustine in Germany, which (for reasons unknown to me) did not wish to obey the provincial Vicar-General of their Order. This was despite the fact that this Vicar-General had been validly elected and approved by the entire German province of the Augustinians. So, these recalcitrant monasteries banded together to elect Martin Luther as their procurator or representative. This role involved him liaising on their behalf with Rome, and endeavoring to settle the various disputes with which they were involved. The choice of Luther for this position was made on account both of his well-known cleverness and sharpness, his promptness to engage in disputes and conflicts, and his expertise in law.

So, Luther travelled to Rome to undertake the task of resolving the dispute within the Augustinian Order in Germany. And he conducted the business with which he had been entrusted with great astuteness and success; so much so that the disputes and divisions which had long existed between the German Augustinians were resolved.

With his business of negotiations completed, Luther remained in Rome for a while. For he was (for some reason) most keenly expecting the Supreme Pontiff to confer upon him the status of a cardinal, on account of his manifest merits (as he saw it) in resolving the dispute among the German Augustinians. Yet this did not happen. When, at last, the frustrated young Luther asked the Pope directly about his advancement, the pontiff responded that he should not press the matter, but rather that he should be content with the Augustinian habit for the time being.

When he heard this response, Luther was inflamed by the most violent wrath and filled with unspeakable fury and indignation. In anger, he immediately departed from Rome to return to Wittenberg.

In Wittenberg, he was soon afterwards awarded the degree of Master of Theology. The historian [Johannes] Sleidanus[5] writes that this degree was procured for him at the expense of [Frederick], the Duke of Saxony. But it seems more likely that those who opine that the expenses of his graduation were covered by the generosity of a

---

[5] Johannes Sleidanus (1506-1556) was a German historian and scholar, and supporter of Luther.

certain wealthy citizen of Wittenberg are correct. This (they say) happened as a result of the urgings of the Vicar-General of the German Augustinians. For it is known that, while Luther was studying in Wittenberg, the Vicar-General of the Augustinians provided for all his financial needs very generously; but, at that point, Luther would still have been completely unknown to the Duke of Saxony. Nevertheless, regardless of how it came to pass, Luther obtained for himself the prestigious degree of Master of Theology.

And Luther had also gained a reputation for being very clever and subtle in disputation and public discourse throughout Wittenberg. But now, driven on by an insatiable desire for even more popular glory and esteem, and no longer content to be a celebrated person in Wittenberg only, he began to visit other places for the sake of acquiring greater fame for himself.

It was Luther's practice to announce certain propositions or theorems, and then to expound them before the public. As part of this "show," he would then invite anyone who wished to dispute his propositions to come forward and speak, and they would hold an impromptu debate before the assembled listeners. He betook himself to Heidelberg, where he quickly gained a great reputation for himself by these displays; so much so that the name of this clever, bold and sharp-tongued young orator was soon on the lips of everyone in that venerable city.

Figure 2: *Luther engaged in public disputation,*
Wittenberg, 1521

III.
The Controversy over Indulgences and Luther's Ninety-Five Theses

In the Year of Our Lord 1517, the Supreme Pontiff, Pope Leo X, exercised the apostolic authority which he possesses over all persons who call themselves "Christians," and mercifully made available plenary indulgences for the temporal punishments due for sins. The condition for gaining such an indulgence was sincere penitence, and a generous giving, in the name of Christ, of something of each person's resources, according to the extent of their wealth and what was possible to them.

But the practical question soon arose: to what cause should the proceeds of these charitable gifts be committed, and to what use should they be applied? There were quite a few who opined that the money should go directly to Rome and be applied to the construction of the splendid new Basilica of St. Peter. This basilica had been commenced under Pope Julius II, but not yet completed. The people who held this view reflected that the building work had been interrupted, and that the vast edifice could not be brought to a fitting completion without very considerable financial resources being made available.

But others asserted that the money should be directed towards funding a large armed force to combat the Turks. For Pope Leo X had already called upon the King of France and many other rulers to contribute resources and assistance to this important cause. The people who held this view believed that, if the funds were directed to establishing a powerful militia, it would be possible liberate the Holy Land from the dominion of the Turks, and to protect Christian Europe from their onslaughts.

Meanwhile, a multitude of these plenary indulgences were given, in honor of the Holy Cross. Those engaged in preaching and publicizing them would have large wooden crosses carried with them. These large crosses were painted red and were set up in locations where great crowds of people could see them, as a means of promoting contributions.

There was no-one who did not recognize the granting of these indulgences to be a most praiseworthy work of mercy. For it resulted both in the remission of many sins, and in encouraging the general populace to give alms generously, according to their means. It cannot be denied that some of those who were responsible for collecting and processing the offerings misappropriated what was entrusted to them and did not properly follow the procedures laid out in the papal documents. However, such regrettable cases certainly did not undermine the integrity and good results of the work as a whole.

Now, it was the established custom in Germany at that time for the preaching and publicizing of papal indulgences to be entrusted to the members of the Order of St. Augustine. But in this instance, it happened that the administration for Germany was delegated to the Prince-Archbishop Albert of Mainz, a prelate who enjoyed the privilege of being an elector of the Holy Roman Emperor. And he, acting upon the advice of certain persons, appointed Fr. Johannes Tetzel, the Preacher-General for the Dominicans in Germany, to head the campaign for publicizing and promoting the indulgences in that country.[6] For Tetzel did seem most suitable for this role, being one of the most celebrated preachers in the country at the time. And Tetzel assigned the task of promoting and administering the indulgences to the members of his own order, the Dominicans.

This situation gave rise to bitter discord, and some members of the Augustinian Order felt indignant at not being assigned responsibility for the promotion and

---

[6] Laing uses varying orthographies for the name of Johannes Tetzel. Here he gives "Sterzen", and a little later "Thetzet." In both cases, an examination of other sources makes it clear that the person in question was the same Johannes Tetzel (1465-1519), a Dominican friar who was the chief promoter of the papal indulgences in Germany.

administration of the indulgences in Germany—since it had customarily been their role. Archbishop Albert himself felt some sympathy with the Augustinians and was well aware of the resentment which had arisen amongst them. It was, arguably, the inability of some members of the Augustinian order in Germany to accept this situation with equanimity and resignation which gave rise to the unrest which led to the catastrophe which followed.

For the Vicar-General of the Augustinians for the German Province at the time, Fr. Johann von Staupitz,[7] considered the matter very seriously. Staupitz was a man of very distinguished abilities and most expert in business matters of all kinds, but he was also subject to fiery anger. He was of noble birth, and there was to be found no-one who surpassed him in eloquence, physical strength, or comeliness of appearance. For all of these reasons, he was held in very high esteem by Frederick, the Duke of Saxony. So, this Staupitz successfully persuaded the Duke that the indulgences granted by the pope were nothing more than a means of extracting money from the poor. He asserted that those who were promoting them and administering them were practicing fraud, to induce people to be separated from

---

[7] Johann von Staupitz (1460-1526) was a German Augustinian. He initially supported and encouraged Luther, but later separated from him and remained loyal to the Catholic Church. Towards the end of his life, he became a Benedictine monk.

their hard-earned money, and so to enrich themselves. Alas, there is nothing so pious and noble that it cannot be made to seem wicked, if interpreted in a sufficiently cynical and negative manner!

When the Duke heard Staupitz persuading him in this manner, he was naturally quite convinced, having no reason to doubt the honesty and veracity of the views being expressed. Indeed, the young Duke was gullible and naïve to accept the words of so wretched a flatterer, who said one thing with his mouth, while he knew something quite different in his heart!

Staupitz was furious that the Augustinians had been deprived of the income from the administration of the indulgences, and so began to portray them as something corrupt, dishonest and worldly. To assist this campaign, he summoned Martin Luther to join him. Now Luther himself, barely *compos mentis* by then, was likewise indignant at the loss sustained by his Order. He wrote a lengthy epistle to Albert, Prince-Archbishop of Mainz (who was also an Elector of the Holy Roman Emperor), dated on the last day of October, in the Year of Our Lord 1517.

In this letter, Luther gravely complained against the notion of the certain remission of sins by means of indulgences. He also enclosed a long compilation of many theorems or theses he had concocted—ninety-five to be exact—arguing against the efficacy of indulgences.

In these theses, he also against the doctrine of purgatory, the sacrament of penance, and many other true and venerable beliefs of the Catholic Church.

It should be mentioned that Luther had already made public these propositions, or ninety-five theses, in Wittenberg. There, he had invited anyone who had any objections to his propositions to come forward and had pledged himself to refuting them. It is to be noted that these propositions were all entirely incongruous with the judgments of the Angelic Doctor, St. Thomas Aquinas, and the views of all other orthodox theological authorities.

Figure 3: *Certificate granting a plenary indulgence, authorized by Pope Leo X, and stating the conditions of the indulgence*, c. 1515

IV.
The Scandal Commences

The news, or rather scandal, of these ninety-five theses of Luther soon reached the ears of Fr. Johann Tetzel, a member of the Dominican Order, who had been acting as the chief preacher of the papal indulgences in Germany. As an expert theologian, Tetzel had also been empowered by the pope to make inquiries into all doctrinal matters concerning the Catholic faith in Germany.

After he had considered Luther's ninety-five theses, he immediately wrote, published and publicly explained his own propositions (some one hundred and six), refuting those of Luther. After this public split concerning doctrine and Church teaching, great unrest began to emerge amongst the people. This was, alas, the commencement and origin of innumerable grievous woes which would scourge the entire length and breadth of Germany.

Luther, who (with the support of Duke Frederick of Saxony) was the cause and author of all this trouble, was conspicuously absent when it came to open disputation with Tetzel and showed no desire to achieve a reconciliation. Rather he displayed himself to be an enemy of peace, and a man born for the destruction of the Catholic faith and the public good, by openly and persistently teaching and defending his doctrines at the University of Wittenberg. But he presented his arguments in such a fawning, sycophantic manner, and filled with so much fake humility and counterfeit piety (even having the audacity to dedicate his work to the Supreme Pontiff, Pope Leo X!), that he won over many sympathizers for himself. Most of these sympathizers were so deceived by his false words and persona that they felt pity and commiseration for him.

Luther declared that what he had written and taught had been disparaged by his foes, and that (as for himself) he desired nothing fervently more than peace, concord, and the salvation of souls! Furthermore, he presented himself as a veritable paradigm of love for and loyalty to the authority of the Supreme Pontiff. Thus, like a venomous serpent, one thing was expressed in his mouth, while the very opposite thoughts lurked in his heart!

Here is the nauseatingly insincere and groveling dedication which this man wrote to Pope Leo X, and which he would read at the beginning of all his lectures:

> "Most blessed Father, I prostrate myself before You, and cast myself down before

the feet of Your Holiness. All that I am and all that I have done, I offer to You alone. As You will, summon me to life, or kill me! Call me to Yourself, or reprimand me; approve me, or reprove me—do unto me, I beg of You, whatever best pleases Your Holiness. For Your voice is the very voice of Christ Himself, who speaks through You alone. If You consider me deserving of death, then most gladly shall I die."

Behold the mendacious words of a guilty and manipulative arch-flatterer! Needless to say, all of this Luther wrote for no other purpose than to allay the concerns of the Pontiff, so that, freed from the scrutiny of the ecclesiastical authorities, and beguiling the faithful into believing him loyal to the Church, he might more easily plot the ruin of the Catholic religion. And so it happened that many learned and upright men come to be deceived into believing that this apparently religious man was not doing anything at all contrary to the faith, but rather that all his activities were directed to helping the Church. And, having been thus tricked by this impious heretic, many began to favor Luther. And some of the most talented poets and orators of the University of Wittenberg turned their invective against Luther's opponents.

The controversy and bitterness which arose about this matter was enough to extinguish in the hearts of many of the people in that area the piety and trust they had previously felt towards the papal indulgences. And the good reputation of Tetzel, who had hitherto been the most celebrated preacher in all of Germany, was severely damaged.

Nevertheless, many of the more expert theologians, who had a clear understanding of the issues and the truth of the situation, began to write against the ninety-five theses of Luther. Amongst these were Master [Johann] Eck,[8] who was the most learned German theologian of the time, and Sylvester Mazzolini, of the Order of St. Augustine, who was also Master of the Palace of the Pope.

Despite the fact that these were men of the highest intelligence and learning, Luther responded with hateful vitriol. He said that Eck was clearly mad and delusional, and that all of his arguments were based on faulty foundations. About Sylvester Mazzolini,[9] he said he was stupefied by his book and could not understand a word of it. Nevertheless, Luther complained that Mazzolini's book contained very few quotes from Sacred Scripture

---

[8] Johann Maier von Eck (1486-1563) was a German priest and theologian, who was a prominent and articulate opponent of Luther's views. He later became archbishop of Trier.

[9] Sylvester Mazzolini (1456-1527) was an Italian Dominican priest and theologian. After serving as a professor of theology for many years with distinction, he was appointed by Pope Julius II as Master of the Sacred Palace.

but was full of citations of St. Thomas Aquinas. And Luther, at this point, audaciously announced that he placed no credence or value whatsoever on the thoughts of the Angelic Doctor but considered them all to be worth nothing!

Mazzolini responded very reasonably by issuing a short but cogent booklet asserting the authority of the Bishop of Rome in matters of faith and doctrine, as the legitimate successor of Peter. But Luther, in turn, published a most scandalous and barely rational letter in reply, in which he stated that, if the opinions of Mazzolini (which were, in fact, perfectly orthodox) were those of the pope and the cardinals, then he could only conclude that the Roman Church was the Antichrist!

V.

The Venom Spreads throughout Germany, and Cardinal Cajetan Attempts to Settle Matters

With such wicked and impious errors of the heretic Luther sending forth deeper and deeper roots throughout Germany, the Supreme Pontiff wrote many letters to Frederick, the Duke of Saxony. He requested and implored him that the piety, love and devotion which he had hitherto always shown to the Catholic, Roman and Apostolic Church he should now set forth clearly, through both his words and his actions. If he wished to do this (the pope counseled him) he would immediately do all that was necessary to put an end to the false, pestiferous and pernicious doctrines of Luther.

Motivated by these urgings from the pope, Duke Frederick did all that he could do to quell and quieten the heresies and schismatic tendencies of Staupitz and Luther. This brought matters to a head. Since the Supreme Pontiff was now involved, he summoned Luther to Rome, so that, on a fixed date, he might respond publicly to the many complaints and allegations against him which were now in common circulation.

Martin Luther did not hesitate to accept this papal summons, which he saw as an opportunity to advance himself. He set to work with great industry, seeking to ingratiate himself with as many leaders and influential people as he could. And so, the matter became a prominent issue all throughout Germany.

The University of Wittenberg, which was already severely infected with the virus of Luther's ideas, dispatched a letter to Pope Leo X, on September 25, [1518.] This epistle was elaborately drafted and employed every trick of vain and specious sophism to convince the Supreme Pontiff that Luther had said or done nothing contrary to the holy Catholic Church. Rather, they argued that he had simply advanced academic propositions for discussion and examination, according to the usual custom of dialecticians and scholastics. In conducting public disputations upon these propositions, he had done nothing unjust (so they said), nor had he said anything deliberately false or unreasonable. Rather (they said), through his disputations and formulations, he had demonstrated them to be true, or, at least, plausible.

After this, Luther went to Rome, in response to the pontifical summons, making a great show of the fact (as he would have it) that he had not let either infirmity of body or the perils of the journey hold him back from obedience to the pope. This time he responded in an apparently reasonable manner and made a display of himself as being apologetic and submissive to the Supreme Pontiff. He requested that His Holiness should send forth judges to Germany, who would be qualified and able to examine the whole issue thoroughly and settle the disputes and differences peaceably.

And so the pope, in response to the request of Luther and the urgings of many members of Luther's party (by whom he was, alas, most wretchedly deceived), showed himself to be humane and merciful. He appointed Cardinal [Thomas] Cajetan[10] to examine the whole matter, and authorized and commissioned him to detect, correct, and—where necessary and demanded by justice and reason—to punish, any heresy he discovered in Germany, among the supporters of Luther.

On the fourth day after the arrival of Cardinal Cajetan in Germany, he interviewed Luther. Now, Luther was at that time feeling protected by letters of support from Duke Frederick of Saxony, and by the assurances given to him by the Emperor Maximilian [I], who had publicly pledged his safe passage.

---

[10] Thomas Cajetan (1469-1534) was an Italian Dominican who served as Master of the Order of Preachers from 1508-1518. A distinguished Thomistic theologian, he was created a cardinal in 1517.

Cajetan met with Luther politely and kindly. He advised Luther in the most civil terms that the Supreme Pontiff requested three things from him, in order that he should be fully reconciled with the Catholic Church. These were, firstly, that he should acknowledge his sins and errors; secondly, that he should do a fitting penance; and, thirdly, that he should publicly declare that he had expressed erroneous views in both his writings and his preaching. He also requested of Luther that he should solemnly undertake not to return to his former errors at any point in the future, and promise not to write or preach anything contrary to peace and unity of the Catholic Church in the future for as long as he lived.

Now, Luther was of an invincibly proud, stubborn and obstinate disposition. Accordingly, he immediately denied that he had ever written or preached anything contrary to his own conscience. O, such a "conscience": for truly, it was such a conscience that a fox might possess—a blinded conscience, and one dedicated to the perpetuation of pestiferous heresy! Since, as Luther asserted, he had never said or written anything contrary to his own conscience, there was (so he said) no error or sin to acknowledge, and no views which he would retract.

Now, Cardinal Cajetan was a most learned man, expert in disputation, and erudite in Sacred Scripture and theology. Citing the Scriptures and the decisions and rulings of various Church Councils, he carefully and patiently undertook to show the numerous errors which Luther had expressed. Luther was perplexed and could not reply to this compelling evidence, so he asked the cardinal to grant him one day in which he could prepare his reply. This Cajetan generously granted to him.

The next day, Luther returned to Cajetan, accompanied by four of the leading officers of the emperor. Luther carried in his hand a letter, which commenced to read. The letter ran thus:

> "I, Martin Luther, of the Order of St. Augustine, declare myself to revere and to embrace the holy Roman Church, in all that I do and in all that I have done, in the past and present, and also in anything I will do in the future. If there is anything whatsoever in what I have said which is contrary to the Catholic Church or its teachings, then I wish and request that it may be entirely disregarded and treated as if it had never been said."

This incident is recorded in the commentaries of [Johannes] Sleidanus—and it is to be noted that this Sleidanus was himself an avowed heretic and supporter of Luther, and so tried to write nothing at all contrary to him or which reflects badly on him. Nevertheless, he also relates this shameful incident in further detail, stating the Luther, after reading this hypocritical letter, placed it into the hands of Cajetan. He confirms also that the letter stated that Luther was perfectly willing to defer to any others who understood the topics and questions better than he. This included, so he wrote, all the doctors of theology at such universities as Freiburg, Basel and Leuven. Luther expressed his willingness to defer to the opinions of the faculty of theology of the University of Paris, whom he praised to the very heavens—as if he considered them the most learned men in all the world!

But the good cardinal, though kindly and well-disposed, recognized immediately that Luther attempted to deceive him and gain time for himself, and to hoodwink him by a combination of subterfuge, sycophancy and obfuscation of the issues. In fact, he saw that Luther's supposed but clearly insincere willingness to defer to the opinions of others was, in fact, a form of mockery and a rouse.[11] He ordered Luther to desist from his diatribe, and not to return to his presence until he was willing to acknowledge his errors clearly and retract them. He told Luther that unless he was ready to do thee three things required of him by the pope, and that if he tried to confuse matters by stirring up fruitless and vain

---

[11] Clearly if the opinions of all the theologians of the universities which Luther named were to be sought on the various questions and issues, the matter would never be properly resolved, but rather become complicated beyond all measure.

disputation, he would have no choice but to apply to Luther the punitive measures which he was authorized to employ by the Church.

But it should be noted that, though Cardinal Cajetan did admonish Luther with this threat of punishment, he sincerely would have preferred to do nothing severe against him. Rather, he strove by all possible means to have him return to the truth of the Faith and to unity with the Catholic Church.

Figure 4: *Cardinal Cajetan and Luther,*
Ferdinand Wilhelm Pauwels (1830-1904)

VI.
The Hypocrisy and Falsehood of Luther's Responses to Cardinal Cajetan

On the third day after this interview with Cardinal Cajetan and Luther had taken place—that is, on October 27, [1518]—when the cardinal had prohibited Luther from coming to see him again until he was ready to comply with the requests of the pope, Luther wrote a letter to him. In this letter, Luther stated that he recognized and acknowledged his error, and he assured Cajetan that he held him in the highest regard, stating that there was no man alive to whom he felt more goodwill. He also promised (with false and hypocritical piety) never to do anything contrary to the holy Roman Catholic and Apostolic Church. But he stipulated a condition to all of this—namely that Luther's foes be prohibited from publishing anything attacking him, in reference to any of his previous errors (which he acknowledged and retracted). [But Cajetan declined to be dictated to by Luther about this.]

Next, Luther wrote to the pope himself, asserting that he would have gladly resolved to live the rest of his life quietly and unobtrusively, according to the rules of the Order of St. Augustine and the Catholic Church—unless Cardinal Cajetan had been so lenient to his enemies, who (so he claimed) had been slandering him.

At this time, Luther also began to write another book in the city of Augsburg, In this work, he claimed that all of the rumors in circulation about him were totally false, and sought to distance himself from all the allegations in circulation against him. In this work, he asserted, not only falsely but also foolishly (as is the custom amongst miserable heretics!), that Cardinal Cajetan had not used a single syllable of Sacred Scripture in his condemnation of Luther's propositions. And he said that when the Cajetan was asked to find a single line of Scripture to support his condemnation of Luther's views, he was utterly unable to think of anything. And Luther made this absurd claim even though it was universally recognized that there was scarcely anyone living who was more learned than Cajetan in the fields of Scripture, theology and philosophy!

When the cardinal departed from Germany and Luther returned to Saxony, the latter recommenced his career in a manner more wicked and impious than before, as if he had become completely oblivious of his own salvation. In all of this, the friendship and authority of the Duke [Frederick of Saxony] added considerably to Luther's arrogance and presumption. He published letters addressed to all and sundry, inviting them to Wittenberg to dispute his propositions publicly. Luther also publicly pledged that anyone who should oppose him or disagree with him would be perfectly safe and secure; and not only that, but he promised that food, drink and lodgings would be freely and abundantly provided (at the expense of the duke) for anyone who made the journey to participate in these disputations.

Oh, how happy and fortunate are those leaders who know how to use their wealth and resources wisely! But how wretched was that leader, the Duke of Saxony, who was deluded and deceived by the dark clouds of the pretended rightness and greatness of Luther! How miserable he was to be led astray by this wicked heretic, this horrendous flatterer, this detestably monster, who was the cause and origin of such a multitude of evils!

For by the monstrosity of the heresy spawned by Luther, England has now virtually perished; Scotland lies prostrate and well-nigh buried; Ireland is in a state of war and woefully oppressed by the heresy of the English; Flanders is reduced to dust and ashes, partly by insane rebels and insurgents and partly by wicked heretics; and, Germany is so gravely vexed and afflicted that the Catholic Faith has become virtually unknown there. France alone remains almost unharmed and safe from the plague of heresy.

Figure 5: *The Legend of Martin Luther*,
16th-century German woodcut

VII.
Luther is Shamefully Defeated in a Public Debate, and Expelled from the Duchy of Saxony

At last, the Holy Roman Emperor Maximilian [I] passed away in the Year of Our Lord 1519. Then Luther took up fully the horns of his evil, for as long as Maximilian had been alive, that foul and despicable monster did not dare to launch any attack the Catholic Church in open and blatant terms. But now he began to rave viciously against the Roman Pontiff, and to preach his seditious heresies without reserve in every place he could. And the black flames of diabolic pride began to flare up in Luther's heart like never before.

The matter was referred to the attention of various princes and noblemen, for they realized that Luther was behaving like a fierce beast, threatening peace and security everywhere. In that same year, a public debate was organized between Andreas Karlstadt,[12] the archdeacon of Wittenberg [and a supporter of Luther's opinions], and [Johann] Eck, who was then a canon of the cathedral at Ingolstadt. It was arranged to take place at Leipzig, which is a great and celebrated city in Germany.

As the day of this public debate drew near, which was June 27, [1519], Luther suddenly involved himself in the matter—although no-one had invited him. He earnestly implored Karlstadt that he should let himself, Luther, take up the case against Eck in his place. But Karlsadt, although he was a supporter of Luther's faction, said that this would not be possible, for he felt it would be unseemly and ignominious for himself to hand over his assigned role as a disputant to another.

Nevertheless, the two men, Karlstadt and Luther, travelled together to Leipzig for the great public debate. As they travelled, they were accompanied by a great mob of men. There men were peasants of the very crudest variety, a veritable cohort of fools, imbeciles and half-wits. Indeed, they would be better described as a band of hooligans or ruffians than a delegation of

---

[12] Andreas Karlstadt (1486-1541) was a lay theologian, who was a professor at the University of Wittenberg, and later became its chancellor. He generally supported Luther's views at this time, but later became even more radical and even rather mystical. Towards the end of his life, he renounced all his academic degrees (three doctorates), and wore the garb of a poor peasant.

rational men! This mindless band made their journey with two or three huge carriages, laden with books and provisions of all kinds.

Meanwhile, the designated opponent of Karlstadt, Johann Eck, had but a single servant as his retinue. Present at the proceedings was also George, the Duke of Saxony,[13] who was a prudent, reverent and thoroughly sound man. He asked everyone concerned that they should conduct themselves in a respectful and honorable manner, and refrain from using abusive and foul language. He exhorted them to be mindful always of God and the truths of the Faith, and to consider this same God and His divine truth as looking upon them as a judge of whatever they said or argued. Moreover, he stressed that they were to say nothing against the Catholic Church, or contrary to its Faith.

O righteous and pious leader, Duke George of Saxony, you shall certainly obtain a place of primacy in the Kingdom of Heaven! For you recognized that the glory of God was to be given precedence over all other concerns, and that fear of God should underpin all our actions.

---

[13] This was George I, known as 'George the Bearded', who ruled the *Duchy* of Saxony from 1500-1539. Frederick, who has appeared several times in this narrative already, ruled the *Electorate* of Saxony from 1486-1525. Although both are described as Dukes of Saxony, they governed different parts of that region of Germany.

The debate began with the question of the freewill of human beings, and then proceeded to various articles of religion. It continued in the most bitter and heated fashion for some ten days. Karlstadt [who represented Luther's views] was miserably defeated, and merited for himself such disdain and contempt that it can barely be described in words. He then realized within his own heart that he was not capable of responding to the convincing arguments of Eck.

And Luther himself did not want to enter into the debate at this point, unless the judgment of the matter was placed in the hands of the ill-educated and ignorant mob of his supporters, who formed the majority of those present as the audience. But this proposal was not supported by the educated people present, who realized that the crowds were completely unqualified to judge the outcome of the debate.

Finally, Luther, seeing that he had no other option, agreed for professors from the Universities of Paris and Erfurt to adjudicate the debate. But when the discussion was resumed before these learned judges, Luther began to find himself frustrated and confounded, and so became inflamed with fury. In this maddened state, he often contradicted himself, and was compelled to refute many of the views he had publicly propounded elsewhere. Thus, it was that Luther found himself wretchedly vanquished and publicly embarrassed. Lamenting his humiliating defeat, Luther withdrew from the debate, and Karlstadt briefly resumed his role as disputant against Eck, to bring the proceedings to their end.

The next day, which was July 15, [1519] the public debate was concluded, and the decision committed to the judgement of the adjudicators. George, Lord of the Duchy of Saxony, a very illustrious man and firmly loyal to the Catholic Church, perceived that Luther was nothing but a cunning imposter and a contemptible heretic, who readily infected simple, gullible and unwise people with the venom of his lies. Therefore, he resolved to punish Luther severely, unless he should immediately depart from his territory.

VIII.

A New Emperor is Elected, and the Commencement of the Diet of Worms

Meanwhile, Frederick, the Duke of the Electorate of Saxony, who favored Luther's cause, became seriously ill. Luther, having been expelled from the territories of Duke George, now hastened to Duke Frederick. There he wrote for the duke a book entitled *Tesseradecas* [or *Fourteen Consolations*], and another on the confession of sins.

At around this time, [1519] the Prince-Electors convened in Frankfurt, to elect a new Holy Roman Emperor. They elected to this role Charles [V], the King of Spain and Archduke of Austria. Charles was then just eighteen years old, and a fine youth of noble character and form, but still inexperienced.

So Luther immediately began to plot and plan how he could deceive this new emperor and win his favor. He gained as a co-operator in this treacherous task a certain wicked, cynical and atheistic man named Ulrich von Hutten,[14] who had written a godless book entitled *The Roman Trinity*. These two scoundrels—Luther and Hutten—plotted together on the most effective way they could lure the new emperor to their cause and separate him from the Catholic Faith.

Luther and Hutten took up a campaign of writing, produce tracts attacking the Supreme Pontiff as well as various persons in leadership in the Catholic Church. Needless to say, these writings were stuffed with every kind of ignominy, infamy, opprobrium and slander.

Luther addressed one of his books to the newly created emperor. This was a fawning work that wrapped itself in the disguise of piety and humility and drew upon the writings of innumerable heretics. It was dedicated to the emperor and the princes of Germany, and recounted all the conflicts and struggles which had ever taken place throughout the course of history between Roman Pontiffs and German emperors, kings and princes. In this way, it aimed at renewing and aggravating all

---

[14] Ulrich von Hutten (1488-1523) was a German knight, scholar and author, who supported Luther's views. In his youth, he had entered the Benedictine monastery at Fulda, but later fled from the monastery to pursue a life of libertinism and debauchery. He died of syphilis, and wrote a book about his horrifying experiences of this disease.

possible animosity and ill-feeling it could between Germany and Rome.

Next, Luther wrote a book entitled *On the Babylonian Captivity of the Church*, which is filled with maledictions, slanders, lies and defamation. In this infamous work, he searches for any and every possible excuse and justification, however ill-founded and false, for attacking the papacy. This work caused Pope Leo X to condemn Luther officially as a heretic.

Now, if Luther was motivated by any genuine desire to do the will of God and felt any true piety, he would have immediately acknowledged and retracted all his errors. But, on the contrary, he immediately became even more obstinate, pertinacious and aggressive. He produced a tract against the pope's Bull of Excommunication against him,[15] to which he dared to assign the title *Against the Execrable Bull of the Antichrist.*

The emperor, Charles V, ordered that all books written by Luther, that worst and most obstinate of heretics, should be consigned to the flames. And he actively undertook to ensure that this was carried out. The merits and virtue of this young emperor are attested to by none other than his son, King Philip II of Spain, who is universally known as the brave champion and constant

---

[15] The bull of excommunication referred to here is *Decet Romanum Pontificem,* issued by Pope Leo X in 1521.

defender of the Catholic Church. The illustrious and holy Philip II, rightly known as the "Most Catholic Monarch," would never grant the slighted concessions to heretics of any kind.

This burning of Luther's heretical books first commenced in the towns in the province of Brabant.[16] This greatly displeased Duke Frederick of Saxony, who did everything he could to convince the emperor that Luther was the very best of men, and extremely holy. The emperor was a youth who had been piously educated and a firm lover of the Catholic Church.

Although he was young, the Emperor Charles was astute and intelligent, and recognized at once in Luther the cunning and duplicity which characterizes all heretics. In the Year of Our Lord 1521, he convoked a meeting of all the princes of Germany in Worms, which is a city of the empire. The meeting [the Diet of Worms] commenced on January 16. The emperor ordered that first of all, they should listen carefully to spokesmen sent by the pope to address the assembly. These identified some forty articles in Luther's book *On the Babylonian Captivity of the Church* which were very clearly heretical. These heretical extracts from Luther's writings were read in the presence of all the princes of the empire.

---

[16] Located in modern-day Belgium.

Among the offending views proposed by Luther was that there were not seven sacraments in the Catholic Church, but only three—namely baptism, Eucharist, and penance. When this new and pestiferous teaching was heard, immediately the good princes were horrified, and their hearts were inflamed with righteous indignation. Indeed, such was the intensity of feeling this aroused that the supporters of Luther were suddenly filled with fear. Frederick, the Duke of Saxony, who was a supporter and protector of Luther, now asserted, quite falsely, that what they had heard read to them had never been written Luther at all! He did this, of course, to escape the hatred, anger and ill-opinion of himself that he saw was likely to arise, since he was known to be a friend of Luther.

Figure 6: Ulrich von Hutten, a German knight and libertine who
died of syphilis, and a co-operator with Luther

Figure 7: Cover of Pope Leo X's *Bulla Contra Errors Martini Lutheri et Sequacium* ("Bull against the errors of Martin Luther and his follower"), 1520

IX.

Luther is Summoned to the Diet of Worms, and his Disgraceful Behavior while Travelling

Martin Luther himself was summoned to the assembly at Worms by imperial decree. On the sixteenth day of March, Kaspar Sturm,[17] an illustrious man who was counted amongst the chief advisors of the imperial court, was sent by the Emperor Charles to Wittenberg, with official letters summoning Luther to the emperor's presence. Having read these letters, Luther, together with a large band of his companions, organized a most extravagant and ostentatious journey. Travelling in a great procession of wagons, Luther and a great multitude of his cronies made their way through the country. One of his companions was a certain Johannes, who had recently been appointed as prefect of the Church of All Saints by the emperor. It was this individual who undertook the arrangements of travel, determining

---

[17] Kaspar Sturm (1475-1552) was a German diplomat and author.

their route in such a way that they visited every single tavern and wayside inn along their course.

The horrendous and shocking spectacle of this band of merry travelers was such that it caused amazement and wonder amongst all who witnessed it and was upon the lips of all the people as an unprecedented scandal. For in whatever tavern or inn they entered, Luther would have copious quantities of wine brought out, and he and his companions would spend the whole day getting drunk, dancing, and making disgusting jokes and playing foolish pranks.

As is the case with many Germans, often Luther and his friends would seem to be perfectly sober as long as they were seated at the table, but as soon as they stood up, it became clear that they were utterly intoxicated, lacking control of their hands, feet and tongues. And if they were not able to control the limbs of their bodies, how much more surely were their brains addled!

Furthermore, so that nothing might be lacking in their debauched merriment, many of those (who, in their drunken state, considered themselves expert musicians) would begin to sing, dance, or pound on musical instruments. A veritable cacophony of clapping and an infernal chaos of so-called dancing would then break out. How beautiful and sweet did Luther imagine that harmony to be, as if he were a new Orpheus! But, in truth, he was more like a debauched Bacchus, returning to Germany in drunken triumph after having plundered the Orient of all its treasures.

All those who beheld these dreadful things were astonished and aghast and were filled with chilling horror. For indeed, it was not merely ridiculous, but wicked, sinister and impious. For here was Luther displaying himself as a depraved monster—all the while still clad in his monastic garb and displaying the tonsure of a professed member of the Augustinian Order, while dancing and singing in a state of the most bestial intoxication.

At this point, the emperor heard the news of this scandal, and immediately sent a message to Luther that he was to desist from all preaching and teaching until he had appeared before him. Nevertheless, Luther, in a manner typical of all heretics, flatly refused to obey, declaring that he recognized no-one as superior to himself, except for God alone. Thus, did he confuse his purely fleshly impulses with divine mandates, and refused to obey anybody but himself.

And the very next Sunday, which was the first Sunday after Easter, our Martin preached openly in the town of Eckernförde, sowing the venomous seeds of his heresy among the common people.

Figure 8: Frontispiece from *Von dem grossen Luterischen Narren* ("On the Great Lutheran Fool"), by Thomas Murner, 1522

X.
Luther's Appearance at the Diet of Worms, and his Expulsion by the Emperor

At last, Luther arrived at Worms, on the sixteenth day of April, [1521] and was received at the guesthouse of [the Knights of] Rhodes.[18] The next day, he was led to the emperor. It was the great Johannes Eck, now Archbishop of Trier and official spokesman of the emperor, who addressed Luther. Using kindly and civil words, he spoke to him thus:

> "Martin Luther, you are being summoned by the His Holy Majesty the Emperor for two reasons. The first reason is to ask you whether you admit that certain books which have been read and examined at this assembly are really yours. The second reason is [if these writings

---

[18] That is, the Order of the Knights Hospitaller of St. John, commonly known at the time as the Knights of Rhodes, and at present as the Knight of Malta.

> are, in fact, yours] to ask if you wish to defend
> the contents of these books."

When Luther heard these words, he was completely astonished, and struck with cowardly terror. The blood ran from his face, and he grew pale. He did not utter a single syllable, for he judged it safer for himself to remain silent than to risk speaking a word he would regret.

So, one of Luther's supporters who had accompanied him—a certain Hieronymus Schurff,[19] a lawyer—requested that the titles of the books in question be read to them. This was done, and Luther perceived that he could not credibly deny these books to be of his own authorship, so he had no choice but to acknowledge them as his own. But, with false humility and true cowardice, he requested some time to be granted to him, in which he could consider the various objections which had been raised against their contents and propositions, and to frame his response. This request for time was generously permitted to him.

The next day, Luther then delivered a speech to the assembly at Worms. First, he excused himself from any fault whatsoever. Next, he stated that his books should be recognized as belonging to two different types

---

[19] Hieronymus Schurff (1481-1554) was a German jurist, who was appointed by Duke Frederick to act as Luther's counsel at the Diet of Worms.

or genres—for some treated questions of doctrine, whereas others were aimed at imparting good morals and conduct. He asserted that in both those works which treated doctrine and those which treated morals, he had nothing which he wished to retract or even to reconsider. On the contrary, Luther behaved as if he had done all things well. Arrogantly and pertinaciously, he proclaimed that he had not sinner or erred in any way.

He discoursed at excessive length, in a manner that was deeply ambiguous, obscure and perplexing, to such a point that all of his listeners became deeply frustrated and profoundly bored with him. This is very typical of all cunning heretics, who strive to frame their erroneous positions in a way which eludes all proper understanding and evaluation. Eventually, the assembly had tolerated as much as they could of this self-righteous but empty diatribe. So, they called for an adjournment, requesting that the proceedings should continue on the next day.

That next day was the second Sunday after Easter. On that day, the noble emperor wrote letters with his own hand to all the princes of his empire. He stated clearly and unequivocally that it was his intention to live as his ancestors had, in communion with the Catholic Church, and to defend that Church as his forefathers had done before him. Moreover, he decreed that Luther was to be treated as a known and infamous villain, and an obstinate and pertinacious heretic. But the princes of the empire, to ensure that civil war did not break out, suggested that Luther should simply be required to acknowledge and retract all his errors, and return to the fold of the Roman, Catholic and Apostolic Church, outside of which there is no salvation.

But, alas, their good and merciful intentions were entirely in vain! For there is no-one more deluded and insane than a heretic, and Luther was like a man possessed by an evil demon. In his diabolic pride, he imagined that no-one thought or behaved correctly, except for those who thought and behaved exactly as he did!

Still, Luther strove to ingratiate himself to the princes. For their part, these princes were by nature inclined to mercy and goodwill. Luther stated that he was ready to accept their advice, and that he accepted the teachings and doctrines of all the Church Councils, with the single exception of the Council of Constance. Now this Council of Constance[20] had condemned the notorious heretic Jan Hus,[21] and ordered his execution by burning. Luther made a weak and partial defense of some of his propositions, but otherwise promised to obey the will of

---

[20] 1414-1418.

[21] Jan Hus (1369-1415) was a Czech priest and theologian. He was condemned as a heretic at the Council of Constance.

the emperor and the princes, making a show of false piety and reverence.

But the emperor saw through this at once, and knew that faithfulness, falsehood and wickedness were united in Luther's heart. He commanded that Luther should depart from his lands within twenty-five days. And this he did, albeit unwillingly.

XI.
Luther's Ever-Increasing and Delusional Arrogance

Following the decision of Emperor Charles V to expelled Luther from his domain, on the 26th day of April [1521], which was a Friday, Luther departed from Worms. Then, on the eighth day of May, the emperor formally promulgated the decree of Luther's exile. In this decree, he commanded that Luther should depart from his lands, and that if he should ever be found within his territory again, he should be seized and arrested. Moreover, he ordered that all of Luther's books should be consigned to the flames, and that, under pain of death, they should never be printed again. It was similarly forbidden to sell or possess copies of books by Luther.

This decree greatly disturbed Duke Frederick of Saxony, who was Luther's protector and supporter. Duke Frederick secretly gave Luther refuge in Wartburg Castle at Eisenach. There the heretic Luther, now also an outlaw, remained in concealment for some time, all the while furiously writing a multitude of new books.

It happened at this time that some of the works of Luther came into the hands of Henry VIII, King of England. That monarch was filled with justified outrage, and immediately took up his pen to write against Luther. With wonderous aptitude and skill, he refuted Luther's propositions. Most notable of all, inflamed with an incredible love for the truth, he wrote against Luther in defense of the seven sacraments.[22] And at the very beginning of this book he pledged himself to be a most faithful champion and defender of the Catholic Church.

But, alas, after he grew old, Henry VIII entirely changed his position. For his queen—a most praiseworthy and pious woman—reached an age when she was no longer able to beget children for him. Alas, how many evils and snares do the foul lusts of the flesh set for incautious mortals! Henry, who had long been a most loyal and loving friend of the Roman, Catholic and Apostolic Church, now suddenly became its most bitter enemy. This was because the pope would not grant him permission to divorce and repudiate his lawful and

---

[22] This book by Henry VIII, the *Assertio Septem Sacramentorum adversus Martinum Lutherum,* is often believed to have been co-authored by St. Thomas More. In recognition of this work, Pope Leo X granted to Henry VIII and his successors the titled of *Defensor Fidei* ("Defender of the Faith").

true wife—a pious woman, to whom he had married for twenty-four years, and with whom he had hitherto lived as a married couple in tranquility, harmony and respectability. Moreover, this woman, his lawful wife, had borne him many children. What was worse—and, in fact, deserving of death—was that Henry wanted then to take another, younger woman as his wife.

It was out of this scandal that schism against the Church first emerged in England. After this schism from Rome, England began to follow heretical doctrines. It is out of this pestilential doctrine of Lutheran heresy that Scotland also has now almost perished, that Ireland is sorely vexed, that France is agitated, and that Flanders was been alienated from its king—in short, that all of Europe has been imperiled!

But I should return my attention to the matter at hand. Luther responded to the objections to his errors so cogently presented by Henry VIII by saying that he was answerable only to the Divine Majesty, and that he couldn't care less if a thousand St. Augustines, or a thousand St. Cyprians, or a thousand Roman Churches, or a thousand King Henrys raised themselves up against him! "Who is this king," wrote he, "with such a small brain and narrow mind, that he wants us all to be subject to the Roman Pontiff?" Thus did Luther write, adding many other similarly inept and impertinent aspersions against the King of England.

Around this time, some of the nefarious books of Luther also came into the hands of certain noble women. These women, misled by Luther's speculations and assertions, were led to discuss theological questions among themselves. One of these women, a certain Argula [von Grumbach],[23] who wished to be seen as an expert or teacher to all the others, began to assume the role of a public preacher! We have heard that the same scandal had already taken also in Scotland, where a certain matron, more audacious than all her peers, had begun to preach to other women.

But why should I use the word "preach?" It would be truer to say that she called down bitter and severe punishments upon all those who (as she would have it!) sinned by refusing to obey the new "fifth Gospel." Now, a certain one of these so-called sinners who happened to be present objected to her preaching, pointing out that it was against the laws and customs of England for a woman to preach. Moreover, she pointed out that St. Paul had explicitly prohibited it in the fourteen chapter of the First Letter to the Corinthians, in which he commands women to be silent and does not permit them to teach.[24]

---

[23] Argula von Grumbach (1492-1569) was a German noblewoman and author, who supported Luther.
[24] See 1 Corinthians 14:34.

This righteous and justified objector to this self-appointed female preacher (who was also a woman herself) continued, saying: "O woman, you are most foolish and presumptuous! Did Christ ever give the office of preaching and teaching to any woman, even His own blessed Mother? Did he make His beloved Mother, the Virgin Mary, the head of His Church? No, He bequeathed it to St. Peter, as St. John relates in his Gospel, when He entrusted Peter three times to feed His sheep. In doing this, He constituted St. Peter as head over His other disciples. We have read," she continued, "the words of St. John Chrysostom explicating this passage, as applying not only to St. Peter but also his successors. And St. Cyprian, in his fifty-fifth letter, writes that all heresies and schisms come to birth because of refusals to acknowledge the one priesthood established by Christ Himself."

Meanwhile, Luther continued his own preaching with an unprecedent level of arrogance. To the great astonishment of everyone who heard him, he declared that the truth of Christianity had been systematically concealed and kept secret, from the time of the apostles until his own times (that is, the Year of Our Lord 1523). Furthermore, it was only he, Luther, who, like a new Messiah, now revealed these long-hidden truths to the world!

At that time, Luther translated the Bible into the German language, and had a vast number of them printed. This translation was filled with innumerable errors. Meanwhile, Ferdinand, Duke of Austria and brother to the Holy Roman Emperor, together with other princes who were loyal to the Catholic Church, ordered all of Luther's books to be consigned to the flames. This decree inflamed the soul of Luther himself with ungovernable fury, and he began to protest in barely rational terms to the Emperor and others.

Many very learned Catholic theologians, motivated by love of God and loyalty to the Church, began to write against the false and inept views of Luther. Amongst these were Johann Eck, Thomas Murner,[25] and Johannes Diemberg—who detected and proved quite irrefutably no less that eighty-seven clear errors and falsehoods in Luther's writings. Other theologians who wrote against Luther's heresies at this time was St. John Fischer, Bishop of Rochester, and St. Thomas More, both Englishmen of the highest learning, who would later both lay down their lives as martyrs.

But Luther, like one who is utterly blind—or rather, like some beast devoid of reason and made rabid with demonic pride—replied by asserting that all the saints, loyal to the Catholic Faith throughout the centuries, had been in error, and that, in fact, the entire Church

---

[25] Thomas Murner (1475-1537) was a distinguished German Franciscan theologian. He was also an accomplished poet, being appointed a poet laureate by Emperor Maximilian I.

had been deluded. Rather, he asserted that it was he alone and no-one else who understood the truth. He went on to say, with blasphemous and insane arrogance, that it was impossible for *him* to be wrong, since (to use his own words), "my doctrine is not my own, but that of Jesus Christ." Luther used these very words in his writings addressed to Henry VIII, King of England, and thus he equated himself with the only-begotten Son of the eternal Father. O, what unprecedented temerity, and what unfathomable impudence—rather, what pitiable insanity, what utter madness! Such words are certainly tolerable to no Christian and to no right-thinking person.

Next, Johann Cochlaeus,[26] a most intelligent man, wrote two works against Luther, one *On the Grace of the Sacraments* and the other *On Infant Baptism.* Luther had barely finished reading the first of these volumes, when he and his companion [Wilhelm] Nesen[27] wrote and published a letter in reply. This vitriolic and bitter piece of writing is filled with scandalous insults, mockery and crude jokes directed against the learned Cochlaeus. So appalling and tasteless is this letter that one can hardly read it without feeling ashamed, and much less can one give this disgusting piece of libel to anyone else to read!

---

[26] Johann Cochlaeus (1479-1552) was a German scholar, humanist, and opponent of Luther. He also wrote extensively on musical theory.
[27] Wilhelm Nesen (1492-1524) was a German scholar and supporter of Luther.

A little later, Nesen, who had helped Luther write this document, drowned himself in the Elbe River, which runs by Wittenberg, apparently struck by guilt at the cruel and scandalous way he and Luther had defamed Cochlaeus. Luther was overcome with black despair at his associate's suicide. But such was his delusional arrogance that Luther prayed over the dead body of his partner-in-crime, firmly but vainly believing that he would be able to summon forth his soul from the infernal darkness of the underworld, to re-animate the water-logged corpse of the unfortunate suicide.

After failing in this attempt, Luther then renewed his vitriolic attacks on the pious and respectable Cochlaeus, calling him a "defender and protector of tonsured monks." Cochaleus, being a learned and capable man, wrote a well-argued book in his defense, on the grace of the Sacraments. He gave this book the title *Against the Cowled Minotaur.*

This whimsical title, [*Against the Cowled Minotaur*] was a reference to a certain absurd interpretation Luther had placed on a strange event which had transpired in Wittenberg. For it happened that a calf had been born there with no hair on its skull, as if it had a monastic tonsure. This calf also had a fold of skin over its head, resembling (very vaguely, to Luther's fanatical and deranged imagination) a monastic cowl. Luther, deluded with his own ideas, took this occurrence as a prophetic omen from God Himself, indicating that those who wore the monastic habit or were vowed to religious life were, in fact, nothing but beasts and abominations. Such was the madness of this heretic, that he perceived confirmation of his own obsession even in the chance events of nature! And what is more, he imagined that all educated and pious men would interpret this phenomenon in the same absurd way that he did.

Shortly after this, in an effort to tear the general populace from the unity and concord of the Catholic Church, Luther took it upon himself to re-write the book of ceremonies of the Church. To add to the confusion, he changed nothing in the customary sacred vestments of the Roman Church. He also changed nothing in the Canon of the Mass, with the exception of removing the memorial of the dead. But this audacious heretic demanded that the Epistle and Gospel be read in the German language. He also ordered that all sacred images should be destroyed, with the exception of those depicting the death and passion of Our Lord Jesus Christ. And he removed all feast days of the saints from the calendar. In addition, Luther took it upon himself to re-write the ceremonies for baptism and marriage, establishing entirely new rites to suit his own "new Gospel!"

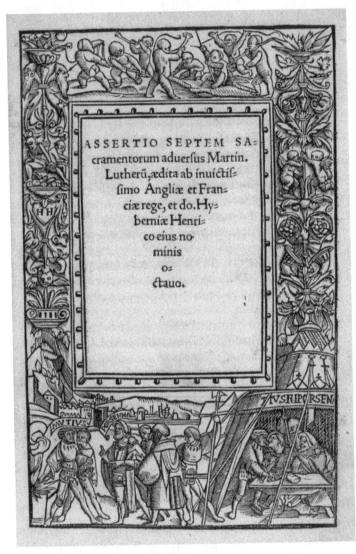

Figure 9: Frontispiece of Henry VIII's *Assertion Septem Sacramentorum adversus Martinus Lutherum,* 1521

Figure 10: Cruelty of the Schismatics in England
(after Henry VIII's apostasy), *Theatrum crudelitatum hæreticorum nostri temporis* (Antwerp, 1587)

XII.
Scandals Committed in the Name of Luther, and Luther's Own Scandalous 'Marriage'

A certain one of the impious heretics who were encouraged by Luther, Leonard Roppen by name, forcibly seized nine vowed religious women, all of noble birth, from the convent at which they resided. He then took them to Wittenberg, which was by then thoroughly dominated by Luther's influence. To make matters worse, this heinous crime was committed during Holy Week, in the days leading up to the most sacred Paschal Triduum. Luther congratulated Roppen on his sacrilegious and horrendous act.

At this point, the Emperor Frederick had been dead for some two years, and there were barely any restraints or limits on Luther's behavior at all. Luther took one of these abducted women, a certain Katharina von Bora, as his wife—or rather, as his partner in adultery. For it is certain that this horrendous sycophant was not able to be validly married. For a marriage is valid only between legitimate persons—that is, between persons who are free to contract a marriage. But Luther had already vowed himself to chastity before God as a member of the Order of St. Augustine and had doubled this commitment through his ordination to the priesthood. Katarina, as a Cistercian nun, was similarly solemnly vowed to chastity before God.

The binding nature of vows is a fundamental principle of both natural and divine law and is confirmed by Sacred Scripture. For in Psalm 75, we read: "Fulfill your vows to the Lord," and in the fifth chapter of Ecclesiastes, it is written: "Do not delay to fulfill your vows to God."

It was well-known that as long as this Katarina co-habited in Wittenberg with Luther, she would also share her company and favors freely with the young scholastics there. Indeed, she was said to be like the proverbial "she-donkey of Jerusalem," which was available for the common use of all.

Figure 11: *Martin Luther and his 'wife,' Katharina von Bora,*
Woodcut, c.1580

XIII.
Bloodshed And Chaos Ravages Europe, Thanks to Luther

At this point, one of the partisans of Luther, a certain [Knight of the Holy Roman Empire] Franz von Sickingen,[28] began to seize the goods and assets of various churches and monasteries, conducting this criminal campaign of banditry and rapine under the pretext of the "New Gospel." This Franz von Sickingen had been incited by [Johannes] *Oecolampadius and [Martin] Bucer.*[29] *These two were both apostate monks, who had betrayed their religious vows and left the Catholic Church under the influence of Luther.*

---

[28] Franz von Sickingen (1481-1523) was a German knight and soldier. Together with Ulrich von Hutten (who has appeared earlier in this history), he led the so-called "Knight's Revolt."

[29] Johannes Oecolampadius (1482-1532) was a German theologian and scholar. Martin Bucer (1491-1551) was a Dominican friar, who, under the influence of Luther, renounced his religious vows. He later moved to England, where he influenced Thomas Cramner. Although Laing described both Bucer and Oecolampadius as "apostate monks," it seems that Oecolampadius, while certainly ordained to the priesthood in the Catholic Church, was not a member of a religious order.

Unfortunately, there are many similar defectors in Scotland at present. Such men are, in fact, nothing but fawning sycophants who feel they can advance themselves more easily by aligning themselves with Luther. Because of this sorry state of affairs, Scotland is now without God, without a king, and without law!

Now, *Oecolampadius and Bucer had both discarded their monastic cowls and condemned true religion, taking Luther instead as their master. Under the pretext of Luther's "new Gospel," they began to seize the property of churches and religious houses on a large scale. And Luther himself added sparks to this fire. For he began to declare that it was perfectly legitimate for the populace to seize the property of monasteries, and that they were fully justified in doing this.*

In this way, Luther incited the common people—who are always gullible, ignorant, and inconstant—*to rise up against their rightful masters, and to violate the laws of nature by rejecting legitimate authority and the principles of private property. Because of this, a revolt among the peasants was stirred up, and countless thousands of these wretches lost their lives, having fallen victims not only to their inherent foolishness, but to the venom of Luther's insanity.*

It was during this war that Antoine, Duke of Lorraine, and his brother Claude, Duke of Guise, obtained a notable victory. But this single victory, though fortunate, was at the cost of the 1,500 ignorant peasants who lost died as a result of their misguided uprising. And the histories written by the French of the whole series of outbreaks of peasant rebellions attest that no less than 26,000 human lives were lost.

By this point in time, virtually all the cities in Germany had become infected with Lutheran heresy. As a result of this, the former academies and faculties of theology were almost all reduced to extinction. Indeed, all fields of learning and philosophy declined most severely. For Luther maintained that the basics of grammar and the rudiments of language were all that were needed to understand Scripture!

Konrad [Wimpina],[30] a most learned man, wrote that 293 monasteries and churches in Germany were destroyed under the pretext of the new "fifth Gospel." These were attacked, looted and despoiled of their sacred and precious possessions by mobs whose hearts were filled with sedition and tumult, under the noxious influence of Luther's errors.

In the Year of Our Lord 1526, the Holy Roman Emperor [Charles V] summoned the princes and electors of the empire to consult regarding sending a military force into Hungary, to defend that nation against the Turks. But many of these German princes had fallen under the sway of Luther's heretical dogmas, and so they consulted with him about the matter and about the course of action they should take. And Luther advised them (absurdly) that, according to his own "fifth Gospel," it was not permissible to take up arms against the Turks, for those who now gave their loyalty to Christ.

---

[30] Konrad Wimpina (1460-1531) was a German scholar and historian, who remained firmly loyal to the Catholic Church.

Because of this, the King of Hungary was left without military aid against the fierce onslaught of the Turkish hordes. Consequently, he lost not only his kingdom but also his life. For, as he fled from the barrage of the murderous foe, he was—alas—thrown from his steed. Landing in a swamp, he sank under the muddy waters and so drowned to death.

See here, O Reader, the fruits and usefulness of this new "fifth Gospel!" See here the damage done by the frauds, cunning and lies of these miserable and contemptible heretics, whose evil is truly equal to that of the demonic minions of hell!

Figure 12: "Fruits of the New Gospel,"
Theatrum crudelitatum hæreticorum nostri temporis (Antwerp, 1587)

XIV.
The Lutheran Heresy is Condemned
by the Emperor

In the Year of Our Lord 1529, all the imperial princes were summoned together at the command of the Holy Roman Emperor. The purpose of this gathering was to examine all matters pertaining to religion. After long discussion, on the 29th day of November, it was resolved that the pestiferous heresy of Luther must be uprooted, and that all should return to the ancient religion of their realm—that is, the religion of the Holy, Roman, Catholic Church. And all the princes at the assembly gave their consent to this wise resolution.

But when the wretched heretic Luther learnt of this, he was utterly enraged. He behaved like a rabid beast, or like one possessed by a malign demon, whose body is an instrument and tool of the devil. Immediately, he produced two books. The first book is imbued with delusional arrogance, and he writes imperiously in the tone of one who considers himself infallible. The second book is written in a tone of patronizing insincerity, as if he is warning his fellow Germans to be mindful of their salvation.

The first book begins thus:

> "I, Dr. Martin Luther, an unworthy servant
> of Our Lord Jesus Christ, say that even if
> the emperor of the Romans, the emperor of
> the Turks, the emperor of the Tartars, the
> emperors of the Persians, as well as the pope
> and all the cardinals, bishops, priests, monks,
> kings, princes, and indeed the whole world—
> yes, even if all of these argued with all their
> strength and power and abilities to refute the
> view that faith without works is what justifies
> us in the sight of God—then, I say, they should
> all be burned in the fires of hell, forever and
> without mercy!"

Behold the words of this demonically proud heretic! Not
only does he place his own misguided judgement above
that of all the learned men and saints throughout the
ages, but he also openly contradicts the unambiguous
words of Sacred Scripture. For the apostle St. James
writes that: "faith without works is dead. Abraham, our
father, was justified by his deeds, by offering his son Isaac
[…]. So, you see that a man is justified by his actions,
and not by faith alone."[31]

And St. Thomas [Aquinas], in his commentary on the
thirteenth chapter of the First Letter to the Corinthians,

---

[31] James 2:20-23

writes: "It is to be noted that firm faith, without charity, can still perform miracles. But if such faith is without [works of] charity, it is without grace, which is the companion of charity. And without that [charity and grace], no-one can enter eternal life."

And St. Paul himself, where he attacks the heretics of his own time in the thirteen chapter of his First Letter to the Corinthians, shows that heretics are able to possess faith without charity. For he writes: "If I have faith enough to move mountains, but am without love, I am nothing"[32]—in other words, those with faith but without charity are not able to enter eternal life.

And such charity is not able to be counted as genuine unless it is accompanied by actions (at least in adult persons.) For St. Paul also described the actions which inherently pertain to charity, when he writes that:

> "Charity is patient, charity is kind: charity does not envy, nor deal perversely; it is not puffed up. Charity is not ambitious, it does not seek its own advantage, it is not provoked to anger, it does not think evil. It does not rejoice in iniquity but rejoices with the truth. It bears all things, it believes all things, it hopes all things, it endures all things."[33]

---

[32] 1 Corinthians 13:1.
[33] 1 Corinthians 13:4-7.

And the Council of Trent, in [the twenty-sixth to] the twenty-ninth canon of its sixth session, wrote in these words:

> "[If anyone shall say, that the just ought not, for their good works which have been done in God, to expect and hope for an eternal recompense from God, through His mercy and the merit of Jesus Christ, if they persevere unto the end in well doing and in keeping the divine commandments; let him be anathema.
>
> If anyone shall say that there is no mortal sin, but lack of faith;] or, that grace once received is not lost by any other sin, however grievous and enormous, except only by that of lack of faith; let him be anathema.
>
> If anyone should say that if grace is lost through sin, then faith is also lost with it; or, if faith does remain, then the faith which remains is not true faith; or if anyone says that if a person who has faith without charity is not a Christian—then let anyone who says such things be anathema."[34]

---

[34] The quote from the canons of Trent given here by Laing has been expanded slightly, to include some very pertinent texts which he omits. It is possible that he did this inadvertently. But it seems also possible that he was assuming that his readers would be thoroughly familiar with the canons in question, and that, for this reason, he did not need to quote them in full.

Out of all of these authoritative references cited above, it is very easily seen that Luther wrote in a way that was not only totally inept, but even insane. For these authorities, and an almost infinite number of other of equal standing, show that faith without works does not suffice for salvation (at least in the case of adults). Yet Luther stubbornly maintains the contrary.

If anyone wished to undertake an identification and itemization of all the errors, falsehoods, calumnies, slanders, absurdities and delirious assertions found in Luther's books and epistles, it would prove to be a virtually endless task. Indeed, an almost infinite number of books would barely suffice to contain them all. Thanks to him, thousands of human beings have been hastened to their graves, and the same number of souls have been dispatched to everlasting perdition!

Yet the doctrines of this madman have now been embraced by the English. And this perfidious heretic curses the holy Catholic Church, the pope (who is the vicar of Christ on earth)—and, in fact, everyone who dares to disagree with him! And his errors are so numerous, foolish and blatant that they are almost unworthy of being refuted. And the man himself is so monstrous and contemptible that even his name is not fit to be mentioned.

O thrice-blessed, four-times blessed, is the person who has escaped infection from the virulent errors of the nefarious Luther!

Figure 13: *Luther, the Devil's Bagpipe,*
Woodcut by Erhard Schoen (1535)

XV.
The Death of Luther

It now remains to say something of the horrendous and sordid death of this pestiferous monster. It is to be noted that the noble house of the Counts of Mansfeld could not reach an agreement among themselves about certain questions pertaining to inheritance and boundaries of land within their estates. So the summoned Luther, who had been born in that area, to act as judge and arbitrator on the matter.

Martin Luther agreed to fulfil this role, and accordingly travelled to Mansfeld, arriving there on the seventeenth day of February, [1546]. After consuming a lavish dinner, at which he partook immoderately (as was his custom) of food and wine, he entered his sleeping chamber, together with his so-called wife (who, as it will be recalled, was actually a nun solemnly vowed to chastity before God.) It was, in fact, Luther's practice always to sleep with this woman, as if they were truly a married couple. On that fateful night, Luther entered his sleeping chamber—nevermore to emerge alive.

About the exact details of his death, various writers differ among themselves. Some say that he arose from bed and went to perform the necessities of nature; and that he then suddenly fell to the ground, dead. Others claim that he died as a consequence of stomach pains he experienced throughout the night.

The family of the Counts of Mansfeld wished to bury him within their own territory, for it was where he had been born. But [Frederick,] the Duke of Saxony, insisted he be buried in Wittenberg So he was entombed there, with great ceremony and pomp, the body being wrapped in a woolen cloth. At his burial, his notorious and disgraceful so-called "wife," Katerina[35]—in fact, a vowed nun, who had made herself into a whore—stood by the tomb, together with his three sons, Johannes, Martin and Paul.

To summarize the proceedings at his burial, two eulogies were given. One of these was in Latin, delivered by Philip Melanchthon.[36] The other was given in the vernacular, by Johann [Bugenhagen].[37] This later speech extolled

[35] The original text at this point reads "*bella et egregia*" (literally "beautiful and outstanding"), but the statement is clearly meant ironically. The English rendition gives the intended sense, without employing irony.

[36] Philip Melanchthon (1497-1560) was a German scholar, who served as professor of theology the University of Wittenberg. He was also a prolific author.

[37] Johann Bugenhagen (1485-1558) was a German theologian. Ordained as a Catholic priest, he initially rejected Luther's ideas, but was later persuaded to follow them.

the supposed virtues and honors of Luther—though he was, in reality, an individual utterly bereft of either virtue or honor.

And these eulogists, as well as the entire funeral, were completely hypocritical, and even a mockery of Luther's own expressed views. For Luther himself had constantly condemned all kinds of elaborate and extravagant liturgies for the dead.

There are some heretics who perhaps will maintain that Luther was a holy man or saint, and worthy of honor in his death. But I cannot find evidence of a single miracle which is credibly attributed to him. [The authoritative Church historian, Laurentius] Surius[38] states that he was, in fact, the most contemptible of wretches who misled countless souls to perdition. Martin Luther died unrepentant, stubborn in his heresy. For this reason, no-one ought to pour out prayers for his soul

[Tommaso] Bozio,[39] a holy, learned and eminently credible man, writes that Luther was perfectly well in

---

[38] Laurentius Surius (1522-178) was a German Carthusian monk, who became a distinguished Church historian and chronicler. His great work, cited by Laing here, was the *Commentarius Brevis Rerum in Orbe Gestarum* ('A Brief Commentary on what Happened in the World'), published 1568.

[39] Tommaso Bozio (1548-1610) was an Italian Oratorian priest, theologian and Church historian. His principal work, *De Signis Ecclesiae Dei* ('The Signs of the Church of God'), was regarded as authoritative compendium of Church history and ecclesiology.

the evening, and found dead in his bed the very next morning—thus this one who had for so many years aroused great motions in the recognized Church of God, was now ironically reduced to utter stillness in the space of one single night.[40]

---

[40] This last sentenced has been paraphrased slightly, to convey the intended sense more clearly.

Printed in the USA
CPSIA information can be obtained
at www.ICGtesting.com
CBHW051813200824
13469CB00042B/405

9 781962 639422